THE LIONS

For Michael Elliott

RONALD HARWOOD

AFTER THE LIONS

AMBER LANE PRESS

All rights whatsoever in this play
are strictly reserved and application
for performance, etc. should be made
before rehearsal to:

Judy Daish Associates Ltd.
122 Wigmore Street
London W1H 9FE

First published in 1983 by
Amber Lane Press Ltd.
9 Middle Way
Oxford OX2 7LH

Printed in Great Britain by
Cotswold Press Ltd., Oxford

ISBN 0 906399 41 6

CHARACTERS

MAJOR DENUCÉ
SARAH
PITOU
MADAME DE GOURNAY

There are also TWO MILITARY ORDERLIES who double as the OLD CARPENTER and the YOUNG CARPENTER, and one woman who occasionally stands in as SARAH's double.

The action takes place mostly in Sarah's rented villa in Andernos, near Bordeaux, 1914–15, and at the battle-front.

ACT ONE   Winter
ACT TWO   Spring

After the Lions was first presented at the Royal Exchange Theatre, Manchester, on 18th November 1982. It was directed by Michael Elliott, with the following cast:

MAJOR DENUCÉ	John Cording
SARAH	Dorothy Tutin
PITOU	Russell Hunter
MADAME DE GOURNAY	Sheila Reid
OLD CARPENTER/ WOUNDED SOLDIER	Tom Harrison
YOUNG CARPENTER/ MILITARY ORDERLY	Richard Gallagher
THE WOMAN	Wendy Gerrard

Other appearances by Nigel Cummings, Sean Curran

A NOTE ON THE PLAY

After the Lions is intended as a companion piece to my other play with a theatrical setting, *The Dresser,* and I shall give them the collective title of *Plays Theatrical.* A third may be added in time but I do not wish to imply anything as grand as a trilogy; it is simply that, in the course of my work over the past few years, the theatre has been my principal preoccupation and it has emerged as a fitting, not to say inescapable, background for themes and variations which I have wanted to explore.

Sarah Bernhardt is an historical figure and so, I suppose, *After the Lions* is an historical play. But I have not attempted to write a chronicle in the traditional sense. I deal with one incident towards the end of her life because that incident seemed to me to express another aspect of the subject matter with which *The Dresser* was concerned. I plead guilty, therefore, not, I hope, to distorting history, but to interpreting events and motives where necessary.

Fortunately for me there is no great detail concerning the periods immediately preceding and following the amputation of Sarah's right leg. We know that doctors in Paris refused to operate; we know that at the outbreak of the Great War she removed to a villa near Bordeaux; we know she was accompanied by her secretary, Pitou, and her maid-cum-companion Madame de Gournay; we know, too, that an Army doctor, Major Denucé, agreed to remove the leg above the knee. Wilfed Owen, serving with the British forces in France, sent a picture postcard of Le Grand Théâtre, Bordeaux, to his cousin, Leslie Gunston, dated 23 February 1915:

> ' . . . You may be interested to know that Sarah Bernhardt has gone through the operation all right. The doctor (Denucé) was the same who "miraculised" upon one of my boys here. I pass by where Sarah lies daily'.

(From *Wilfred Owen, Collected Letters,* London, 1967.)

Of her convalescence, her unsuccessful struggle to walk with an artificial limb, her efforts to return to the stage, there is only fragmentary evidence. She did, however, indeed visit the French soldiers at the front shortly after her operation.

Little is known of the private lives of Pitou, Madame de Gournay and Major Denucé. In biographies of Sarah, Pitou is always mentioned. He is invariably described as 'faithful', 'meticulous' and 'fussy'. He is written about only in relation to his famous employer and emerges as a devoted servant in keeping with the known, documented facts. But the dramatist has licence to invent and embroider where the scarcity of fact bleaches the more vivid human colours.

Even so I feel duty-bound to acknowledge my debt to several authors who have written about Sarah Bernhardt and whose insights have quickened my imagination: James and May Agate, Lysiane Bernhardt, Reynaldo Hahn, Marie Colombier and Maurice Rostand. Sarah Bernhardt's autobiography, *My Double Life,* was, of course, invaluable. *Sarah Bernhardt* by Maurice Baring (London, 1933) was of particular importance to me. I am, however, especially indebted to Joanna Richardson whose fine biography *Sarah Bernhardt* (London, 1959) brilliantly illuminates the actress's character and talent, and whose delightful shorter work, *Sarah Bernhardt and her World* (London, 1977) was, for its text and splendid pictures, the most helpful of all.

Ronald Harwood
Liss, August 1982

ACT ONE

Winter.

The drawing room of SARAH*'s rented villa, 'fin-de-siècle', over-decorated: Oriental carpet, Mexican sombreros, feather parasols, trophies of lances and daggers, a host of Buddhas, Japanese monsters, Chinese curios, ivory work, bronzes, jackals' and hyenas' heads, panthers' paws. There is a silk-lined coffin, a desk with a telephone, chairs, a divan covered in skins, a table with a phonograph, a camera with a cloth and a magnesium flash.*

The sound of sea.

Lights.

SARAH *is seated in a wheelchair, her right leg bandaged and extended. She is heavily made up and wears a bright red wig. She is attended by* MME DE GOURNAY. MAJOR DENUCÉ *is replacing his stethoscope in a medical bag.* PITOU *watches a little apart from the others.*

DENUCÉ: Above the knee.

SARAH: So be it.

DENUCÉ: You are certain? Above the knee.

SARAH: Since there is nothing else to be done, why ask my opinion? Will you make the necessary arrangements without delay?

DENUCÉ: Wish I was convinced.

SARAH: Convinced or not, do as I ask.

DENUCÉ: These last weeks have had some experience of amputation. In months to come no doubt more. Youngsters, of course, bullet wounds and gangrene, results not always —

SARAH: Is it my age?

DENUCÉ: Certainly a factor.

SARAH: Major, I am asking you to remove my right leg for one reason and one reason only: so that I can return to work. Not to prolong my life, but to allow me to work. I must

       act. I must go to the battlefield, I must comfort our brave
       soldiers at the front. I must work.

DENUCÉ: The risks —

SARAH: If I die, so be it, but my only chance of ever acting again
is to have my leg cut off. Two doctors in Paris have
already refused. They wept at the thought of maiming
me, I the divine Sarah — [*a stab of pain*] I need a man of
steel. A soldier. You are my last and only hope. Telephone the hospital. Make the arrangements.

DENUCÉ: Consider consequences. One leg. Artificial limb not
easy. Sticks. Crutches.

SARAH: Yes, but after the amputation I hope people will say it's
better to see Sarah with one leg than not at all —

DENUCÉ: As what? Forgive harshness. One leg. See you as what?

SARAH: In the theatre it's not the illusion of sight that matters,
but the kindling of the imagination. Second-rate actors
may be beautiful, athletic, even look the part, but I can
give you the very essence of a life in my own terms. I
created the role of a sixteen-year-old boy, the Duke of
Reichstag, the eaglet, when I was fifty-six years old. I
never had a more authentic triumph.

DENUCÉ: True. Saw you. Such grace. Extraordinary.

SARAH: When I act it is my spirit which shines through. And I
have an unquenchable spirit.

       [*She weeps.* PITOU *draws* DENUCÉ *aside.*]

PITOU: Pathetic old hag, isn't she? Speaks in quotations from
her press-cuttings. I've been her secretary for years. She
gets loopier and loopier. I've seen it happening. Chop
the damn thing off. Give us some peace.

       [SARAH *recovers a little.*]

SARAH: I dare to believe I'm capable yet of great things, and I
am fortified in the face of this awful affliction by my art.
But I cannot exercise my art in pain. Take away the
pain.

DENUCÉ: Can't guarantee success.

SARAH: Our professions are remarkably similar.

DENUCÉ: Do my best.

SARAH: Do better. Work miracles.

DENUCÉ: Grave responsibility. Can't even guarantee that afterwards you'll stand upright.

SARAH: Then I shall have plays written for me in which I sit on a throne.

[*Pause.*]

DENUCÉ: This evening. To Bordeaux. Ambulance at six. Operation tomorrow, a.m., early.

SARAH: Thank you. And may I ask you one more favour?

DENUCÉ: Anything. Ask. Do.

SARAH: Stop talking like a telegram.

[DENUCÉ *laughs.*]

DENUCÉ: Comes from training dogs. Hobby. And Army, of course. Short, sharp commands. Habit. Apologies.

SARAH: Accepted stop. Must ask further question stop. Regards Sarah.

DENUCÉ: Not used to being teased.

PITOU: But you like it, don't you, you like it. Here, doggy-doggy-doggy, here doggy-doggy, good boy, good boy. Down.

SARAH: [*to* DENUCÉ] Pitou. He's been my secretary for years. He's perfectly pleasant when we're alone, and he makes me laugh, but he's becoming —

[*She winces with pain.*]

PITOU: Beg, beg.

SARAH: [*to* DENUCÉ] There is something that worries me deeply. Pitou, shut your ears.

[PITOU *sticks his fingers in his ears.*]

Will I be shaved?

DENUCÉ: What?

SARAH: Shaved, shaved, you know very well what I mean. A young actress once told me that being shaved was more unpleasant than the operation itself, but then I think it was something other than her leg that was being removed.

DENUCÉ: Shaved! See what you mean. No. Not shaved. Not necessary.

SARAH: All right, Pitou.

[*She mimes to him to remove his fingers and he does so.*]

PITOU: What a ridiculous thing to ask a doctor. I'm sorry. I couldn't help hearing. What does a doctor know about

such matters? You ask a priest whether or not you'll be
saved.

> [SARAH *stares at him uncomprehending, laughs, but
> then winces with pain.*]

[*to* DENUCÉ] Not many people can make her laugh. I
once made her laugh in Toronto. That's quite a feat,
making someone laugh in Toronto. She gave me an acting
lesson. Horror. Passion. Laughter. Tears. Very comic.

SARAH: Pitou, be quiet. This is serious.

PITOU: So are horror, passion —

SARAH: [*interrupting*] Is there anything else for which I should be
prepared? I don't like to be surprised.

DENUCÉ: You'll be asleep. Anaesthetic.

SARAH: I know that. I didn't think you intended to allow me to
sit up and watch while you sawed through the bone.

PITOU: He's an army doctor, you never know.

SARAH: What a wonderful experience this will be for me. The
main action of the drama occurs while I'm asleep. Very
unusual. I hope you have a steady hand.

> [*A pause.* DENUCÉ *begins to cry.*]

DENUCÉ: Can't do it, can't do it, can't —

PITOU: Oh my God, not another one. You should've gone to that
English doctor. The English don't cry.

DENUCÉ: Cannot cripple a goddess.

SARAH: How touching.

DENUCÉ: Saw you first as Marguerite Gautier. I was twelve.
Thirty years ago.

SARAH: Not so touching.

DENUCÉ: Don't ask me to amputate.

> [*He weeps.*]

PITOU: Yes, a man of steel.

SARAH: [*to* DENUCÉ] Come to me.

> [DENUCÉ *goes to her and kneels. She comforts him.*]

DENUCÉ: Apologize. Unprofessional. Unmanly. Unsoldierly.

> [*He weeps.*]

SARAH: We must all play our part. Your role is to amputate my
leg. All your distinguished colleagues tell me you are a
fine surgeon. I came here especially to find you. This is

not the sort of house I would normally inhabit. You should have seen the decorations. Some people's taste is extraordinary. And will it be easier for you to know that I shall be grateful? The pain invades my waking and sleepless hours. Nine years of pain. Sometimes I have wanted to wrench the leg from its socket with my bare hands.

DENUCÉ: Your portrait above my bed. Next to Salomé.

SARAH: Salomé?

DENUCÉ: First pet. Black labrador.

> [PITOU *laughs, makes a note.*]

You stricken. You. Of all people.

SARAH: You'll tell your grandchildren: I gave Sarah relief from pain by removing her leg. And it's been a much admired leg. [*a stab of pain*] Poets have written odes to the way I walked. 'Queen of the Attitude', I was called. Were it not so swollen now, so ugly and diseased, once removed it would make a fine exhibit for a side-show: Sarah's leg, sawn from her body by Major Denucé. Don't cry. You are doing me a great service. Isn't this typical? The story of my life. I am the one in pain, yet I am called upon to comfort others.

PITOU: Typical. I don't ever remember you doing it before.

SARAH: [*to* DENUCÉ] There, there. [*She takes his hands.*] A surgeon's hands, a magician's hands. How beautiful they are, how —

> [*A terrible silence.*]

Filthy! They're filthy! Look at the nails, they're black with grime. Call yourself a doctor? Get away from me. I've never seen such dirty nails in all my life. Don't dare touch me. Have you been patting your dogs? Pitou, see that he washes his hands.

> [*At speed, overlapping:*]

PITOU: At once, immediately, come along —

DENUCÉ: Let go of me —

SARAH: He must wash his hands —

PITOU: Come along, you heard what she said, soap and hot water for you, my boy —

DENUCÉ: My hands are not dirty —

SARAH: The germs, I'll die of septicaemia —

DENUCÉ: A bruised nail, not dirt —

SARAH: Go and scrub those revolting fingers clean —

PITOU: A bath, you must have a bath. [*calling*] Run the bath, run the bath! Here, boy, here, boy, here —

DENUCÉ: [*to* PITOU] Let go of me!

SARAH: [*to* MME. DE GOURNAY] Take me away, I can't bear this, such blackness —

PITOU: Into the bath immediately, clothes and all, good boy, good boy —

> [MME DE GOURNAY *wheels* SARAH *off quickly. The instant she is gone,* PITOU *lets go of* DENUCÉ, *relaxes, sits, makes a note in his notebook.*]

DENUCÉ: [*enraged*] Nearly struck you. Hard. Hate to be touched.

PITOU: You know what I think? I think she's insane. What worries me is, is it catching?

DENUCÉ: Don't like being grabbed. Don't like being touched.

PITOU: One has to humour her.

DENUCÉ: A bruised nail, that's all.

PITOU: She always exaggerates.

DENUCÉ: In the mess. Cracking walnuts with a hammer.

PITOU: Insane. No wonder she's on the list of hostages the Germans want to take if they enter Paris. We had to get out. The government insisted. That's why we're here. And do you know the reason? When the Germans invited her to appear in Berlin, they asked what her terms were. She replied: Alsace-Lorraine. Asking for trouble. I wish they would take her hostage. No one would pay the ransom.

DENUCÉ: Lost a button. [*He looks for it.*] Gold button with regimental coat-of-arms.

PITOU: Why do we bother with her? Do you know the main attraction of this area? A sand-dune. When the wind blows, the sand gets in your hair, in your mouth —

DENUCÉ: Can't go round improperly dressed.

PITOU: And it could all have been avoided, if only I had been more vigilant. I blame no one but myself. And her.

DENUCÉ: Help me look.

PITOU: For want of a mattress a leg is lost.

DENUCÉ: Don't understand a word you say —

PITOU: Then I'll explain.

DENUCÉ: Ah. Found it. [*He picks up the button.*]

PITOU: Did you ever see her as Floria in *Tosca?*

DENUCÉ: No.

PITOU: Rio de Janeiro, the night of 9th October, one thousand, nine hundred and five years after the birth of Our Lord, Jesus Christ. Disaster. Nine years ago, nine years of disaster. *Tosca*, she as Floria, the last act, the last scene. She is on the battlements, pacing and passionate. 'Yes,' she howls, 'I killed your Scarpio, killed, killed, do you hear?' They send an officer. He returns. 'Yes,' he says, 'Scarpio is dead.' And then Spoletta looks up at her on the ramparts and shouts, 'Ah! Devil! I will send you to join your dead lover!' She is still for a moment. She looks down on them. She speaks. 'I go willingly.' She cries. And then, so quickly, seeing is believing, in one spectacular leap, she throws herself off the platform and falls to her death — to great applause, of course. God knows how many times she made that leap, landing — unseen by the audience — on a great mound of mattresses. A famous leap. Floria's leap. On that night, 9th October, 1905, in Rio de Janeiro, there were no mattresses. Someone had forgotten to set them. She landed on the hard floor, on her right knee, her cry of pain drowned by the tumultuous cheers. Nine years ago. Nine years of increasing pain. Why didn't I check the mattresses? Why didn't she?

DENUCÉ: Accident. Inexplicable. Shall I make the arrangements?
[DENUCÉ *goes to the telephone.*]

PITOU: 'I go willingly.' Ironic. Haunting. We have a phonograph record of her in *Tosca*. I play it often, God knows why. Always in moments of stress. Over and over again. [*He laughs.*] 'I go willingly.'

[DENUCÉ *lifts the telephone and taps the receiver.*
SARAH *wheels herself in;* DENUCÉ *immediately
replaces the receiver.*]

SARAH: I apologize. My courage is skin-deep. In my head a sudden
black and awful chasm opened. Before me flashed brief
but vivid images, playing cards riffled by a conjuror. A
knife, hacked flesh, pulsing blood, a face masked, my
dismembered limb lying beside me, the knee level with
my eyes, a dead lover, a still-born child. Always I have
tried to harness my terror to gain repose, but in that
moment I faltered. My fear insulted you. I am through
the blackness now. I want nothing but to be free of pain,
and to face the future. I will be calm and practical. I
shall go willingly. Please make the arrangements.

[MME DE GOURNAY *wheels* SARAH *towards the exit,
but* SARAH *stops her.*]

[*to* PITOU] Send a telegram to my son, in Paris —
'Maurice my darling. Tomorrow they are cutting off my
leg stop. Spread the word stop. Sarah is looking for left-
legged parts. Love Mama.'

[MME DE GOURNAY *wheels her out.* PITOU *whistles
tunelessly.*]

DENUCÉ: You annoy me.

PITOU: We must all play our part.   *

[DENUCÉ *goes to the telephone and lifts the receiver.*]

DENUCÉ: [*into the telephone*] Hospital Bordeaux urgent. [*to* PITOU]
Extraordinary woman.

[PITOU *takes up a sheet of folded newspaper and
begins to cut a pattern.*]

PITOU: She's not a goddess, you know. She's an old, sick
woman, nothing special. Shall I tell you something
about the Divine Sarah? She is not divine at all. She is of
the earth, earth-bound. She is her own *axis-mundi*.

[*He continues to cut the newspaper.*]

Snip-snip, snip-snip. We are talking about a mad
woman. Have you noticed the coffin? Do you know what
she does? She lies in that coffin, a black muslin veil
covering her face, she lies in her coffin to learn her lines.

Have you ever heard such madness? And that's not the only reason she lies in the coffin. Once, at night, I came by chance into the room and she was not alone. You wouldn't think there's room for two in a coffin, but she could make love in a wash basin. And probably has.

DENUCÉ: [*into the telephone*] Doctor Vandal. Denucé. Confirm surgery. a.m. Good.

[*He replaces the receiver.*]

[*to* PITOU] Operation tomorrow, 0700. All arrangements made.

[PITOU *unfolds a string of paper men and snips off the leg of one of them.*]

[*Blackout.*]

[*In the darkness, voices are heard from a phonograph:*]

OFFICER: 'Scarpio is dead!'

[*Angry shouts.*]

SPOLETTA: 'Ah! Devil! I will send you to join your dead lover!'

SARAH: 'I go willingly.'

[*A brief pause, then the sound of the phonograph hissing and clicking.*]

[*Lights.*]

[*The hissing and clicking continue.* MME DE GOURNAY *is seated, using scissors to cut a black silk stocking just above the knee. She does this to two or three stockings, then begins to stitch the upper piece together, discarding the lower part.* DENUCÉ *is adjusting the strap of an artificial limb.* PITOU *is at the phonograph, staring into space.*]

DENUCÉ: Stop that noise.

[PITOU *removes the arm from the record and switches the phonograph off.*]

PITOU: The cheers drowned her cries.

DENUCÉ: No more, if you please. Don't want her upset. Delicate moment this.

[PITOU *goes to a table piled with bills and correspondence. Somewhere a hand-bell rings. All are alert.* MME]

                    DE GOURNAY *hurries off.* DENUCÉ *quickly hides the*
                    leg and tries to look casual.]

PITOU: Yes, a delicate moment this.

                    [*He whistles tunelessly.* MME DE GOURNAY *returns.*]

MME DE G: She'll be another few minutes. She says she wants to
                make an entrance.

PITOU: Of course.

                    [DENUCÉ *uncovers the limb and works on it again.*]

MME DE G: She's an inspiration, a wonderful woman. So brave, joking
                all the time, talking of the future, of visiting our brave
                soldiers in the front line — [*She stops; goes close to* PITOU.]
                — I think I shall have to give in my notice. I'll never be
                able to cope. I'm a maid not a nurse. I'm squeamish. I
                faint easily. My knees go to water. She talks about her
                stump. I — [*to* DENUCÉ] Oughtn't she to have a trained
                nurse? I can't change dressings, bandages. The smell,
                the responsibility, the sight of it. I can't bear the word
                'stump', it conjures up such a lamentable picture. I feel I
                shall faint.

PITOU: [*quietly*] I wish you would.

                    [MME DE GOURNAY *returns to cutting and stitching*
                    stockings.]

MME DE G: I believe I've been misled.

PITOU: Why should you be different from anyone else? [*to*
                DENUCÉ] You won't get paid for this, you know. She's
                bankrupt.

DENUCÉ: Yes. You said.

PITOU: Just thought I ought to warn you. At least we'll halve the
                bill for shoes. She's done for. And if the newspapers are
                anything to go by, we're all done for. I haven't been paid
                for eight months, two weeks and four days. And I'm her
                secretary. I'm the one who does the paying so you can
                imagine how short we are if I haven't paid myself.

                    [*He laughs.*]

DENUCÉ: Want her to take two steps today. That's all. Two.

PITOU: Two steps do not make a waltz.

DENUCÉ: Extraordinary healing power. Stump already like leather —

MME DE G: Please don't —

SARAH: [*off*] Stand back. I'm advancing at full tilt.

> [DENUCÉ *quickly hides the leg. All three stand in expectation.* SARAH *enters on two crutches. She wears a dressing gown. She is triumphant and out of breath, but looks magnificent.*]

There! I have written a poem to commemorate this occasion.

> [*She hobbles to a plinth or pedestal, hands her crutches to* MME DE GOURNAY *and balances herself.*]

Ode to a maimed goddess by Sarah B. aged — [*She mumbles comically.*] It's very short.

'Do not weep for Sarah B.

Wipe your eyes and you will see

An actress whom the world will beg

To act again upon one leg.'

> [*Silence.*]

I realise it's not Racine but there's no need to look quite so critical. I will not have sad faces. A new life has been given to me and I intend to make the most of it. I am free of pain almost for the first time this century. I shall act again. I shall visit the battlefield. My powers of magic are restored. I will once more inspire and cause men to forget their earthly existence. [*to* DENUCÉ] Have you got my new leg?

> [DENUCÉ *uncovers the leg.*]

Why were you hiding it from me?

DENUCÉ: Thought sight of it would shock.

SARAH: Shock? A wooden leg shock? My dear, if you'd ever played Sydney, Australia on a Monday night you'd know what shock is. [*She examines the leg.*] Amazing. Much prettier than the makeshift one you fitted in the hospital. Not as shapely as the real thing but less troublesome, one hopes. How is one to give the illusion of gliding, I wonder? When I am finished as an actress, I have only one ambition: to be a concièrge. One is always sitting. Well, come along, Major, proceed. Fit the damn thing and launch me. Turn your back, Pitou, or leave the room.

> [PITOU *turns his back but from time to time peeps and makes a note in his notebook.* DENUCÉ *and* MME DE GOURNAY *help* SARAH *to sit. They gather round to fit the limb. While the fitting is taking place*:]

Pitou, send a telegram to Mrs. Campbell in London: 'Leg removed. Stop. Very Happy. Stop. Love Sarah.' And send another to Edmond in Paris. 'You have written a play for a man with a long nose stop. Why can't you write one for a woman with one leg stop. Love Sarah.'

> [*She cries out in pain.*]

DENUCÉ: Too tight?

SARAH: The pressure —

DENUCÉ: [*to* MME DE GOURNAY] Loosen bottom strap —

> [MME DE GOURNAY *has to turn away. She puts her smelling salts to her nose.* DENUCÉ *does what ever is necessary to* SARAH*'s leg.*]

[*to* SARAH] How does that feel?

SARAH: Like a wooden leg.

DENUCÉ: Comfortable?

SARAH: That's a ridiculous question.

DENUCÉ: Not painful.

SARAH: No. Not painful.

DENUCÉ: If you'll allow me.

> [*He lifts her up.*]

SARAH: How strong you are.

DENUCÉ: Now. Ready?

SARAH: As ever I shall be.

DENUCÉ: Right. We begin. Lift the leg.

> [SARAH *tries.*]

SARAH: I can't, nothing happens, I — what did you tell me in hospital?

DENUCÉ: Imagine crossing legs. Right over left. Remember? You did well.

> [SARAH *tries again. The leg moves under the dressing gown.*]

Good. Good.

SARAH: It's the oddest sensation, like trying to turn the pages of a book with one's teeth.

DENUCÉ: Again. Several times.

[While she raises and lowers the leg several times under the dressing gown:]

SARAH: It was most mysterious. I continued to feel pain in the leg for six days after it had been amputated. Not the pain of the operation, but the pain of my tubercular knee, as if it were still there. I didn't dare tell you, Major. I was terrified. I believed I would be forever haunted by that excruciating ache, like an animal gnawing at my nerves and tendons, a spectral pain in my amputated leg. Then, on the seventh day, it rested. I dared to look down for the first time at my stump, saw what you'd left me, and the sensation receded, like a slow, stately exit to thunderous applause. I cursed my imagination and welcomed reality. I touched the stump to confirm the truth of dismember- ment. I said to myself over and over again: 'There is no leg, only a stump, no leg, only a stump, only a stump, only a stump —'

[MME DE GOURNAY faints. DENUCÉ goes to revive her. PITOU laughs.]

Isn't that typical? I'm the one in distress and she faints.

PITOU: But then you are not squeamish.

SARAH: Is that usual, Major?

DENUCÉ: Oh, yes. Even medical students faint —

SARAH: No, no, I mean imagining pain in a leg one no longer possesses.

DENUCÉ: Have known it. Not every patient has the experience.

PITOU: Not every patient has the imagination.

MME DE G: *[coming to]* I am so sorry, so terribly sorry —

SARAH: I have no sympathy with people who faint. If I fainted every time I heard or saw something unpleasant I'd be perpetually comatose. How you were ever a dancer puz- zles me. Such a physical profession. Is it true that dan- cers' toes bleed like squashed tomatoes and that they dip them in methylated spirits to harden them?

MME DE G: I never did.

SARAH: That is no answer. How long must I go on raising this piece of wood under my dressing gown? It looks quite obscene.

> [*She laughs, and although the laugh is dangerously near to hysteria, it is infectious.* PITOU *and* DENUCÉ *laugh too.* MME DE GOURNAY *gets herself a glass of water. The laughter stops. Silence.*]

DENUCÉ: Want you to stand now.

> [*With difficulty,* DENUCÉ *and* MME DE GOURNAY *help* SARAH *to her feet. They keep hold of her.*]

SARAH: A remarkable piece of wood. I am again upright. Let me see if I can manage alone.

> [*They let go of her. She sways but keeps her balance.*]

DENUCÉ: Bravo.

SARAH: But how shall I ever move? I can't stand on a stage motionless like this all night. I can't move.

DENUCÉ: Patient. Be patient. Takes time.

SARAH: I haven't the time. I want to walk now. I must be able to walk through the ranks of our army. I must stand before them, a symbol of all they are fighting for.

PITOU: [*to* DENUCÉ] She means it, you know, she means it. Mad, quite mad.

SARAH: I must walk unaided today. I shall will myself to succeed. Teach me, Major, how to walk.

DENUCÉ: [*to* MME DE GOURNAY] Cushions. [*to* SARAH] Now, exactly as when sitting down. But imagine kicking a ball with right leg.

SARAH: Splendid. I have never kicked a ball in my life but now I will proceed to imagine it.

> [*She tries to take a step. Nothing happens.*]

Of course, I have seen a ball being kicked. One winter, in England, outside Manchester, when I was visiting my friends the Agates, I was driven in my carriage down winding lanes, the naked branches of the trees my guards-of-honour. It was bitterly cold and I was wrapped in furs. Presently, we came upon a field with two teams of men ranged against each other, disputing possession of a ball. We paused to watch. They were covered in mud. For more than half an hour, with wondrous skill, they kicked the ball this way and that. I adore cricket, it's so terribly English. Well, Major, I'm imagining that I am playing cricket but nothing seems to be happening.

DENUCÉ: Kick the ball.

> [*She tries; still nothing happens. She forces a laugh.*]

Kick the ball, woman!

> [*She is stung by his tone of voice. Eyes closed, with enormous will, she tries. The others are all trying too, their legs twitching with effort.* SARAH *moves, almost falls.* DENUCÉ *rushes to take her hands.*]

SARAH: Don't hold me. Keep your distance.

> [DENUCÉ *steps back. Again the act of will. With great effort, she starts to move, barely takes a step then falls.* PITOU *is the first to reach her, the others a second later. She lies absolutely still. They get her to the divan.*]

Undo the leg. I'm suffocating.

> [*She faints.* DENUCÉ *revives her.*]

MME DE G: [*to* PITOU] She is allowed to faint.

DENUCÉ: [*to* MME DE GOURNAY] Get the chair.

> [*She goes.*]

SARAH: For Jesus Christ's sake, remove the leg.

> [DENUCÉ *removes the limb.* SARAH *moans softly with relief, then whimpers quietly. Silence.*]

I must earn money somehow.

DENUCÉ: First time. Only first time.

SARAH: You know nothing. How can I walk on that monstrosity? I can only limp, and I shall never limp. Throw it away, make splinters of it, sell them as souvenirs, there'll be an income in that — I'm so hot — I'm burning — don't speak to me — I don't want sympathy or encouragement or good advice — I shall never walk again — I'm fainting —

> [MME DE GOURNAY *returns with the wheelchair while* DENUCÉ *revives* SARAH.]

DENUCÉ: You will walk. You will work.

> [SARAH *turns on him savagely:*]

SARAH: I'm a cripple.
                  [*Silence.*]
              I don't want to die before I'm dead.
PITOU: [*quietly*] Who does?
                  [*He whistles tunelessly. Pause.*]
DENUCÉ: Had hoped to find better time to say this. Off to front
              tomorrow. Must take my leave. Wanted to know you'd
              managed first steps. Wanted to know you'd walked.
              Extremely sorry. Army doctor. In peace time, mostly
              malingerers. In war, God knows. Unlikely chance put
              you in my care. Great honour. High point. Please. Try
              again. Please. Walk. Comfort to me in battle, thought of
              you restored.
                  [*Silence.* DENUCÉ *turns and goes quickly.* SARAH
                  waves MME DE GOURNAY *away and she too goes.
                  Pause.*]
SARAH: Any offers?
PITOU: No.
SARAH: Nothing at all?
PITOU: Nothing.
SARAH: What will become of me? What was the purpose of all
              that pain?
                  [PITOU *turns his back on her, makes a note.*]
              If I'm to be denied plays, I must continue to act. I must
              act. People will still want to hear me. And see me. Won't
              they? I shall recite. I will give concerts, scenes, speeches
              from my most famous roles. I can still give the very
              essence of a life — The Eaglet, The Lady of the Camelias
              — I can still — help me, Pitou, help me — lying on a
              bed, why not? Marguerite Gautier, the final scene, I can
              still — the curtain rises — I am discovered reclining in
              white, camelias at my breast —
                  [*She falls into the dying attitude of Marguerite
                  Gautier.*]
              'I am dying, Armand, but I am so happy and my joy
              conceals my death. You will speak of me sometime,
              won't you?'

[*The light changes. A solitary violin plays a sentimental theme.*]

'Armand, give me your hand. I assure you it's not difficult to die. I'm not suffering anymore. It seems as though life were pouring out of me. I feel so well. I never felt so well before. I'm going to live! Oh, how well I feel!' [*She 'dies'.*]

PITOU: [*ineptly*] 'Marguerite! Marguerite! Marguerite!' [*He 'screams'.*] 'She's dead! My God, what's to become of me?' [*He 'weeps'.*]

[*Lights return.* SARAH *looks at* PITOU.]

SARAH: It's a whole new career. Isn't it? [*Pause.*] Pitou?

[*Silence.* PITOU *whistles tunelessly.* SARAH *stares into space.*]

[*Blackout.*]

[*In the darkness* MME DE GOURNAY *screams in pain.*]

[*Lights.*]

[PITOU *has been writing out cards and filing them but has stopped at the sound of the scream.* MME DE GOURNAY *enters, clutching her arm and deeply upset.*]

MME DE G: I am giving in my notice.

PITOU: Who screamed?

MME DE G: I'm leaving. I should like to be paid.

PITOU: So should I —

MME DE G: I want what I'm owed. I want it now. I want no more excuses. I'm not staying here a moment longer.

[*She sniffs her smelling salts.*]

PITOU: Why did you scream?

MME DE G: She struck me with her walking stick —

PITOU: Hard?

MME DE G: I'm in pain.

PITOU: You must have done something to annoy her.

MME DE G: She's become violent and dangerous and — [*breaking down*] — disgusting.

PITOU: You're sure it wasn't a playful tap?

MME DE G: Look, look at the mark. There's a welt.

PITOU: There'll be another one if you don't control yourself. What happened?

MME DE G: All I said was that I refuse to accompany her. I don't want to go to the battlefield. I don't want to see any more limbless, helpless human beings. I haven't the stomach.

PITOU: And she struck you.

MME DE G: She just sat and stared in black silence. So I said the whole idea of going to entertain the troops was ludicrous.

PITOU: And then she struck you?

MME DE G: I said she wouldn't inspire the soldiers, she'd demoralize them.

PITOU: And she only struck you once?

[*Somewhere a handbell rings.*]

MME DE G: That sound drives me mad. I go to bed hearing it, I wake up hearing it, I hear it in my nightmares. And by the time I've answered it, she'll likely be asleep. I hate her. Who does she think she is? She spills her food, takes no care of herself —

[SARAH *wheels herself in. She looks old and neglected.*]

SARAH: [*to* MME DE GOURNAY] Didn't you hear me ringing? Get out of my sight.

[*She waves* MME DE GOURNAY *away with her walking stick.* MME DE GOURNAY *runs off.*]

That woman is a disaster. Do you know what she said? She said I'd demoralize the soldiers, that I'd lose France the war.

[*She lapses into gloom.*]

PITOU: I have to be harsh with you. Your behaviour is less than first rate. Allow me to say that a little effort is required. You talk of going to visit our brave soldiers, of inspiring them, but you do not have the bravery to inspire yourself.

[*No response.*]

Very well. Do not go to the front. I shall send a telegram to Major Denucé informing him the visit is cancelled. For my own part, I shall breathe a sigh of relief. I am not addicted to travel. I long for a life without movement.

Shall I cancel the visit?

    [*No response.*]

We must make other plans. Shall we return to Paris?

    [*No response.*]

Shall I make you laugh? Horror, passion —

    [*Half-heartedly he simulates the emotions. No response.*]

Evidently not. So be it. Then I must ask you to do as you're told, allow yourself to be treated like a recalcitrant child. And to that end I must ask you not to strike your servants.

SARAH: Strike? Strike? Whom did I strike?

PITOU: Madame de Gournay says you struck her. She showed me a mark —

SARAH: Struck her? I? Did she say that I struck her? She is a congenital liar. I simply made a dismissive gesture with my walking stick and she happened to get in the way. She is terribly accident-prone. It is the story of my life. I have always been maligned.

PITOU: She has given in her notice.

SARAH: Good.

PITOU: She wants to be paid.

    [*Silence.*]

SARAH: What will become of me? [*Pause.*] Why have I suffered all this pain? For what? What has been the purpose?

PITOU: The purpose was, I thought, to rid yourself of pain.

SARAH: I have rid myself of a leg. I have rid myself of possibility. I am weak, dreadfully weak. I have so little energy.

PITOU: You have enough to make dismissive gestures with your walking stick.

    [*Silence.*]

SARAH: Infirmity is terrible for actors.

PITOU: It's pretty bad for audiences too.

    [*Silence.*]

SARAH: I want to talk to you intimately. I regret not doing so more often but we are seldom without company. And you have always been different when we're alone. Will you listen to me without banter?

[PITOU *whistles tunelessly.*]

Listen to me.

[PITOU *stops whistling.*]

I will give recitals. I will play my most famous scenes. And I must go to the battlefront. I must give the soldiers respite. That is a duty, an obligation. But I am haunted by a dreadful, silly anxiety which plunges me into darkness. The anxiety is this: how will I travel?

PITOU: How will you travel? As you've always travelled, I suppose. By motor car, I suppose, by private train, I suppose, by ocean liner, I suppose —

SARAH: Yes, but how will I change platforms at railway stations? I am old. I have so little strength. How will I mount gangways? One can't be wheeled up flights of stairs. My crutches exhaust me. They make my armpits throb with pain. I would have to be carried, but how, by whom? I'm frightened of becoming a piece of useless baggage labelled 'Not Wanted on Voyage'.

PITOU: My point of view precisely.

SARAH: There must be some way of transporting me. At the back of my mind an idea hovers, a memory, a ceremony, a great crowd —

PITOU: Allow me to say, the time has come for a quiet life. The war won't last long, if the newspapers are anything to go by. Why not return to Paris, and there remain? Stationary. A fixed point. A monument. Immovable. Immortal. And once settled, you may think of doing one piece in one theatre for one hundred years. No more movement. No more travelling.

SARAH: No more travelling. [*Pause.*] If only I could recall. Glory. A shaft of sunlight.

PITOU: It's winter now.

SARAH: I despise old age.

PITOU: Allow me to say —

SARAH: Don't lecture me. Make me laugh rather. I haven't laughed for weeks. I want so much to laugh. Make me laugh.

PITOU: Whenever you say that, I feel as though I've just sucked on a lemon.

[*She smiles faintly.*]

SARAH: Humour me. Dispel the gloom. I know you think I'm mad. You always have. Humour me, Pitou.

PITOU: I offered. The moment has gone. Let us play our game instead.

[*He collects up two sets of white pieces, which he sets out on a board.*]

SARAH: Please. Horror. Passion. Laughter. Tears.

PITOU: No, no, no, no.

SARAH: You were so comical as Armand. 'Marguerite, Marguerite, Marguerite!' Please.

PITOU: No.

SARAH: Please, Pitou. Horror. Humour me. Pitou, please make me laugh. Show me your friendship. Make me laugh. Laughter's a sign of friendship.

PITOU: No.

SARAH: You're a miserable wretch. You're trying to make me kill you, but I won't do it. [*Pause.*] I never laughed as much as I laughed in Toronto. Horror, passion, laughter, tears. For an old woman thrown on the refuse heap. Horror. Please, Pitou.

[*Reluctantly, he tries to simulate the appropriate expression. She smiles affectionately.*]

No, no, bigger the gesture. Yes, yes, but open the mouth wider. Wider. Like this. [*She demonstrates.*] You're hopeless. Now, passion.

PITOU: I can't do passion.

SARAH: Of course you can. Let your hands play over your body. [*She demonstrates.*] Don't be a spoilsport. Show me passion.

[*He shows half-hearted passion. She begins to laugh a little.*]

You see how difficult it is to act? You're dreadful, really dreadful. Laughter, now, come, let's laugh.

[PITOU *tries ineptly.* SARAH *lets out a spendid, tinkling laugh. They both laugh now,* PITOU *falsely,* SARAH *convincingly.*]

[*abruptly*] Tears. Cry.
> [PITOU *tries to cry.* SARAH *laughs genuinely.*]

Weep, weep, my dear, weep.
> [PITOU *tries.*]

Weep. You're such an amusing man —
> [SARAH *lets out a glorious wail.* PITOU *tries to imitate*
> *her. She laughs. They both weep.* MADAME DE GOURNAY
> *runs in.*]

MME DE G: What is it, what's happened, have the Germans entered Paris?

SARAH: Can't you see we're in the middle of a conversation?

MME DE G: I'm so sorry, so terribly sorry.

SARAH: You are the most insensitive creature. [*to* PITOU] I was just beginning to enjoy myself. What does she want?

PITOU: [*to* MME DE GOURNAY] What do you want?
> [MME DE GOURNAY *steels herself.*]

MME DE G: My wages.

PITOU: [*to* SARAH] Her wages.

SARAH: She may leave my employ after we return from the front.

PITOU: You may leave —

MME DE G: I do not want to go to the front.

PITOU: She does not —

SARAH: I heard her. Now I understand why she failed as a ballet dancer. She has no sense of the higher purpose.

PITOU: Without wishing to take sides, the higher purpose is all very well, but there is a small matter of the lower reality.

SARAH: What reality? My only interest is to defeat reality.

PITOU: I'm pleased to hear it, because I'd be interested to hear your plans for defeating your lack of money, your abundancy of debt and your imminent bankruptcy.

SARAH: *Et tu, Brute.*

PITOU: You have had no income for months. You live on your credit and you have no credit. You are penniless.

SARAH: Money is irrelevant.

PITOU: Money is irrelevant only to those who have it, among whom you are not presently numbered. You must sell your jewels.

SARAH: Never.

PITOU: You must do something. This is certainly no time to be charitable, however worthy the cause. Forget about our brave soldiers. Make only one more journey. Return to Paris. Give your recitals, open a school of acting, horror, passion, whatever, but let us come to rest.

SARAH: I must go to the battlefield. Artists are the torchbearers of civilization.

PITOU: It's difficult to hold up a torch while standing on one leg.

SARAH: If one has been privileged as I have been privileged, one is beholden to repay.

PITOU: Beholden, I see, beholden, and are we lesser mortals who only have two legs also beholden? Beholden to die in penury, to starve, to be weighed down by — we have lives, too, you know.

SARAH: [*to* MME DE GOURNAY] He's showing off again — leave us —

PITOU: No, this concerns her. She doesn't want to go, I don't want to go, only you want to go, and you are unable. How will you present yourself to the Army? Will you crawl through the trenches? Will you walk their ranks on crutches — ?

> [SARAH *is suddenly consumed with impotent rage. While she talks she hurls things at* PITOU, *or uses her walking stick to smash anything that is near.*]

SARAH: Parasites. Why do you hate me so much? What have I done that you should hate me?

PITOU: Hate you? Stop that — hate you? — I've given you more than half my life — don't — we could get money for that — [*to* MME DE GOURNAY] She's having a brainstorm —

SARAH: The two of you suffocate me in hatred. You begrudge me every breath I take. [*to* MME DE GOURNAY] And you are a catastrophe.

PITOU: We'll have nothing left.

> [SARAH *stops her destruction. She takes off her wig and flings it aside. Her hair is white beneath.*]

SARAH: I am old and poor and defenceless. I need support, not loathing. They have cut off my leg. I cannot even go to the lavatory alone.

> [PITOU *picks up the pieces of a broken object and tries to fit them together.*]

PITOU: [*distressed*] I wonder if we can claim for willful damage on our insurance.

SARAH: I am an actress. I have to travel. My physical presence is my passport. I have lived in dread all my life of being incapacitated. They say you must have gift and talent, but health is — [*She breaks off.*] Send a telegram to Harry Houdini in the United States. 'Houdini, you do such wonderful things stop. Could you bring back my leg for me? Signed Sarah.'

PITOU: You're not serious?

SARAH: I have never been more serious in my life. He does the impossible and I want the impossible.

PITOU: As who does not?

> [*Silence.*]

SARAH: Wheel me back to my grave. I may as well die.

PITOU: Shall I send for a priest?

> [SARAH *is suddenly alert.*]

SARAH: The Pope.

PITOU: The Pope?

> [*He makes a gesture behind her back to indicate total insanity.*]

SARAH: The Pope, the Pope, His Holiness the Pope —

PITOU: I doubt he'll come at such short notice —

SARAH: Stop behaving like a clown. The Pope. I remember now, the ceremony, wait, listen, let me think, he has a word for it, what does he call it?

MME DE G: [*quietly*] Purgatory.

SARAH: In Latin, in Latin —

PITOU: I've lost the thread of this conversation —

> [*Pause.*]

SARAH: *Sedia gestatoria.*

PITOU: Sounds like a bad Italian actress.

SARAH: All Italian actresses are bad. Pen and pad.

> [PITOU *gives her a pen and pad. She begins to sketch rapidly.*]

Don't you remember how the Pope entered St. Peter's?
We were there. I was at the very front.

PITOU: I was at the back.

SARAH: A portable throne. He was carried on the shoulders of his
Swiss Guard, seated on the *sedia gestatoria*. Such glory.
Sunlight. Why can't I be carried on a portable throne?
My own *sedia gestatoria*? I will be lifted by strong, hand-
some, young warriors so that all the army, the hosts of
Gideon, may see me. Find a carpenter. Have him
construct this for me to sit on.

> [*She gives* PITOU *the sketch she had made and begins to
> wheel herself out.*]

[*to* MME DE GOURNAY] On my dressing-table put boot-
black and unctions.

MME DE G: What about your wig?

SARAH: I do not want to tell you again: it is not a wig, it is a trans-
formation. Wigs are vulgar. [*as she goes*] And they say
something to the Holy Father as they carry him, something to do with glory. What is it they say as they carry
him?

MME DE G: Am I to take you for your walk?

SARAH: That is the last thing they say.

> [*She laughs and wheels herself off.*]

PITOU: What do they say about glory? I'll tell you what they say.
They say the glory passes. *Sic transit gloria mundi.*

MME DE G: And I thought I was so privileged. My acquaintances
thought so too. How privileged you are, they said. One
particular friend observed I would not be a maid but a
lady-in-waiting, attendant to an empress, the most
famous, beloved and glamorous woman in the world.
Glamorous. The smell in her room is degrading. In the
mornings, when I enter with her tray, I retch. I have
always been rather fastidious, but she has no self-
respect. She is not greatly enamoured of washing. She
wears the same under-garments for three or four days.

> [PITOU *stuffs his fingers in his ears.* MME DE
> GOURNAY *raises her voice.*]

She snores. I can hear her snoring in my room through the wall. She snores with her mouth open, jaw sagging, tongue lolling. I have to go in and whistle to make her stop. I have to whistle!

> [PITOU *whistles tunelessly.* MME DE GOURNAY *shouts at him.*]

She farts! She is old and cruel and dirty. The divine Sarah smells of stale scent and not the odour of sanctity.

> [*Pause.* PITOU *removes his fingers.*]

PITOU: In future, do not be coarse. I will not have talk of her nether garments.

MME DE G: She's so — so ordinary.

PITOU: Yes, but the Gods whisper in her ear and not in ours.

MME DE G: I thought taking the job would be an inspiration. I've never had the slightest encouragement for anything I've done in my life. My ex-husband said I could do nothing right. But I'm not someone to be disparaged. My father was Superintendant of the Municipal Baths in Lyons. He wasn't rich but at least he had the prestige of the title. I am as much of a person as she is.

PITOU: Yes, and to a Turk Mozart is noise. Do you want your wages? Or will you stay? In this house the persons who are servants never leave. They are dismissed.

> [*He takes out his wallet, counts out some notes and offers them to her.*]

MME DE G: I've nowhere to go.

> [*The handbell rings.*]

PITOU: Time for her walk. The garden is looking particularly bleak at this time of year. The trees bare, the soil frost-hard, and the wind ice. The sand is blowing off the dune and the sea rages.

MME DE G: What am I to do?

PITOU: You are to hear gun-fire and your eyes will smart with the smoke of battle. And when you are old you will be able to say you served her in peace and in war, and that will make you extraordinary. Wouldn't it be paradise if the world were just?

[SARAH *wheels herself in. She has a play text in her hands.*]

SARAH: [*to* MME DE GOURNAY] Why do you never come when I ring? Are you punishing me? Is it that you enjoy seeing me helpless? I need my spectacles. Where are they? Find them.

[MME DE GOURNAY *looks for* SARAH*'s spectacles.*]

[*to* PITOU] I have been so encouraged by the thought of my portable chair, I am alive with excitement. I have had such a splendid idea. I shall do a speech from *The Eaglet* for the soldiers. The one on the battlefield. 'And all the arms — the bloody arms, I see' —

[MME DE GOURNAY *brings* SARAH *her spectacles.* SARAH *puts them on and consults the text.*]

If necessary I shall read it.

[*She searches the text.*]

Yes, here. [*to* PITOU] Find me the cloak I wore. In the chest. The white cloak. [*to* MME DE GOURNAY] Help me.

[MME DE GOURNAY *helps her. She assists* SARAH *to a plinth which* SARAH *leans on.* PITOU *brings her the cloak and helmet.*]

Around my shoulders. I shall wear it over a very plain grey dress. Drape it for me.

[MME DE GOURNAY *and* PITOU *help* SARAH *with her cloak.*]

I've lost the place — yes — here — I shall need my glasses — do you think it's ridiculous me playing a sixteen-year-old boy? Tell me honestly, is it ridiculous?

[*She looks at them for some reaction but gets none. Abruptly she launches into the speech; she starts by reading it but soon lays down the text, and removes her glasses.*]

'And all their arms, the bloody arms I see
Arms without hands, the stumps outstretched to me.
Oh young soldier, with your ashen face,
Forgive me, Oh forgive me! Pray you, grace!'

[*Lights change. The distant sounds of war.*]

'Look not upon me with your murdered eyes,

Accusing me, Ah no! Spare me your cries.'
                [*The sounds of war louder.*]
'My agony has put their woe to rout.
The groans are stilled. And oh, I hear a shout!
Where on the grassy plain woe loomed so large,
Lo, phantom heroes lead a phantom charge!
[*a great cry*] Glory!'
                [*She stands frozen. The sound of war dominates.*]

                [*Blackout.*]

                [*The sounds of war fade to become distant. Torrential
                rain dominates.*]

                [*Dim light.*]

                [*Like a strange eastern caravan, SARAH's procession
                crosses the stage: first, PITOU, under an umbrella;
                then, SARAH (a double), seated on her portable throne,
                carried by TWO MILITARY ORDERLIES. She too, is
                sheltered by an umbrella, as is MME DE GOURNAY,
                who brings up the rear.*]

                [*The sound of cheering. The rain is incessant.*]

                [*The procession crosses and exits. The cheering fades.
                'The Nightingale Song' is played on a solo harmonica. A
                pause, then PITOU re-enters, running under his umbrella.*]
PITOU: I've found him! I've found him! Over here! Over here!
                [*A sudden light on DENUCÉ. He lies propped up on a
                stretcher or a bed, his head bandaged. He stares blankly.
                There is a brazier near him. The TWO ORDERLIES
                carry on SARAH, followed by MME DE GOURNAY.
                PITOU leads them to where DENUCÉ lies. There is much
                shaking off and closing of umbrellas, warming of hands.
                SARAH quickly removes her gloves and takes hold of
                DENUCÉ's hands. He does not respond.*]
MME DE G: The smell of pus is disgusting.
PITOU: They call this place The Morgue. Used to be a school.
                Now they bring the dying here.

SARAH: Be quiet. He'll hear you.

PITOU: He'll hear, but he won't understand.

MME DE G: I'm going to vomit.

> [*She retches.*]

SARAH: [*to* PITOU] Take her out. Leave me alone with him. Call
me when the soldiers are ready.

> [PITOU *and* MME DE GOURNAY *go with the* TWO
> ORDERLIES.]

Major, do you know who I am?

> [*A solo* TENOR VOICE *now sings 'The Nightingale
> Song', accompanied by the harmonica.*]

TENOR: 'Nightingale, nightingale, do not sing tonight,

My men are weary from battle,

Let them rest before they fight.

Nightingale, nightingale, keep a silent watch,

Give my soldiers a blessed sleep,

At dawn again they march.'

> [SARAH *listens for a moment.*]

SARAH: Give me a sign you know who I am. You did me a great
service. They tell me the shell exploded almost on top of
you, and that you're lucky to be alive. Speak to me. Give
me a sign. Say that you know you are lucky to be alive,
and that you want to live.

> [*Pause.*]

Wherever I have gone today I have heard that song, but
I cannot catch the words. [*She listens.*] When I was a
child, a difficult, wayward child, I once said to a Mother
Superior, 'I didn't ask to be born.' She slapped me very
hard, asked God's forgiveness and slapped me very hard
again. I shall slap you in a moment.

> [*Pause.*]

Surely you remember me. I made you wash your hands.
I am senile and gaga now. I am an old and crippled
woman. No worse: I am an old and crippled actress. But
the secret is I'm still that difficult, wayward child within.
Two beings. I called my autobiography *My Double Life*.

> [*Pause.*]

Give me a sign. Show me the life within.

> [*Pause.*]

A man I once loved told me we are duty-bound to live.
He was cruel and gave me pain. But the pain, he said,
was a sign of life. Better to suffer than to die, he said. He
was a playwright. His plays were full of death and despair.
Art has a lot to answer for. If life is so awful, why do we
cling to it so? Speak. Give me a sign.

> [*The song continues to be played on the harmonica. The
> rain is incessant.*]

What is needed is courage and will. I've had the riches of
the earth, fame and adoration and reward. But you must
survive without your name writ large, without helpers,
without fanfares. Nevertheless. Show me that you want
to survive.

> [*Pause. Distant guns.*]

Listen to these words. I've never known anyone who
wasn't moved by these lines. Except the Australians.

> [*Gently she turns* DENUCÉ's *head so that he looks at
> her.*]

'O France, when thou art prone and bound,
Beneath the tyrant's ruthless heel,
A voice from the deep caves shall sound
And rive thy chains of steel.'

'The exile watching wave and sky
Shall raise a voice that men shall hear
Like words that in a dream drift by
Above the darkened sphere.'

> [*Above the rain comes the sound of soldiers, like an
> expectant audience in a theatre.*]

'O'er newer races Time doth weld,
They like a thundercloud shall break;
And if the quick in sloth be held,
The ashamed dead shall wake.'

> [DENUCÉ *looks blankly at her. The soldiers begin to
> clap and stamp their feet. They chant, 'Sa-rah! Sa-rah!
> Sa-rah!'*]

You are not alone. You are alive. You must not want to die. Take strength from me. See in me a body bereft but a spirit indestructible. But I also need encouragement. Give me a sign.

[*No response.* PITOU *and the* TWO ORDERLIES *come to her.*]

PITOU: Two thousand men stamping and calling your name. It won't be long before they tear the place apart.

[*Pause.* SARAH *nods to the* TWO ORDERLIES. *They are about to lift her when* DENUCÉ *suddenly makes a short grunt that sounds either like 'ache' or 'wake'. He reaches out a hand, which* SARAH *grasps.* DENUCÉ *grips her tight and seems to smile.* SARAH *also smiles. The soldiers' shouting turns into a chant: 'Sa-rah! Sa-rah! Sa-rah!' The sound grows and grows continuously.*]

[*Blackout.*]

[*The chant turns into wild applause and cheering.*]

[*Lights.*]

[SARAH *stands in a pool of light, supporting herself between the* TWO ORDERLIES. *She drinks in the ovation, acknowledging the cheers.*]

[*Blackout.*]

END OF ACT ONE

ACT TWO

Spring.

The villa.

SARAH: [*in the dark, very loud*] I never had a more authentic triumph.

[*Lights.*]

[SARAH, *lying full stretch on a chaise-longue and looking glamorous, is on the telephone.* MME DE GOURNAY *is cutting out clippings from newspapers and pasting them in a scrapbook.* PITOU *is busy with the camera that has a cloth and a magnesium flash attachment.* MAJOR DENUCÉ, *head bandaged, is knitting with difficulty. He has recovered physically but requires all his concentration to co-ordinate. Often he wears a lost, distant look and, from time to time, a vacant, foolish smile.*]

[*into the telephone*] A triumph, a great triumph. Two thousand men stamping and shouting my name: Sa-rah, Sa-rah, Sa-rah!

DENUCÉ: Sa-rah, Sa-rah, Sa-rah —

SARAH: [*continuing on the telephone*] What? Carried. Carried. On a portable throne. A throne. *Throne.* [*to* MME DE GOURNAY] The Major's dribbling. [*into the telephone*] You would have been proud of your poor old mother, Maurice. I recited and talked and made them laugh. They lost themselves and I lost my voice. And have you seen the newspapers?

[*She snaps her fingers.* MME DE GOURNAY *brings her the scrapbook.*]

'Sarah Enlists', 'Sarah Goes to War' — too disarming. I brought cheer to the soldiers and reminded the world of my existence. The offers will come flooding in, you'll see. No. Just the servants and Major Denucé. My surgeon,

the man who did the dreadful deed. I've brought him
back here to recuperate. He was shock-shelled or whatever they call the scars of war. What do you mean,
caviar? Surgeon, dear, surgeon! [*She listens*] How much?
Of course. Immediately. Don't worry. But Maurice,
why is it that you never telephone? Why don't you visit
your poor mother? Hello, Maurice, Maurice, hello.

[*She replaces the receiver.*]

We've been cut off. In more ways than one. Pitou.

[*She beckons* PITOU *to her.*]

Send Maurice ten thousand at once. He is in need.

PITOU: So are we.

SARAH: Send it. [*to* DENUCÉ] I was talking to my son, Major. His
father was a prince. I feel so well. Soon, soon, those
good-for-nothing playwrights will put pen to paper.
Sarah can still work wonders, they will say, and they will
chivvy their dull brains into creating vehicles for me.
Vehicles in which I sit.

PITOU: The camera is ready.

SARAH: I'm so happy today. It's wonderfully warm. I do believe
spring is here at last. I can smell the pine trees. The sea is
calm and soothing. But I am restless. I feel Venus is in
the ascendancy. I want to travel.

PITOU: May I ask a favour? Will you allow me to be photographed with you? Playing our game.

SARAH: Of course.

[*He helps her to stand.*]

My dear little Pitou, you are really very beautiful.

[*He helps her towards a plinth on which is set a sort of
game of draughts.*]

Your jacket is disgusting. With all the money I give you,
you can at least be clean.

PITOU: Which you give me? Which you promise me, you mean.
How am I to send money to your son? We have no
money.

SARAH: Oh, you're so pedantic.

PITOU: Will you sell your jewels, your precious stones?

SARAH: No. Never. They are all I have.

PITOU: [*to* MME DE GOURNAY] I will show you how to take the
            photograph.

MME DE G: I've never taken a photograph before.

PITOU: It's quite simple.

SARAH: I feel nineteen again. [*Pause.*] Well, twenty.

                        [PITOU *puts* MME DE GOURNAY's *head under the
                        cloth.*]

MME DE G: Everything's upside down.

SARAH: I feel I have a future.

PITOU: [*to* MME DE GOURNAY] There is nothing to it. Any fool
            can take a photograph.

                        [*He shows her how the camera works.*]

SARAH: The future, yes, the future. Silence! I am about to issue a
            proclamation. [*She hums the opening bars of the 'Marseil-
            laise'.*] The future lies in moving pictures. I shall make
            films. Films are modern sorcery. In films, I shall walk,
            sit, stand and run. Future generations can judge me.

PITOU: Eleonora Duse is making a film.

SARAH: She was always headstrong.

                        [PITOU *takes up his position at the plinth. He and*
                        SARAH *use pointers to push the pieces in their game of
                        draughts.*]

PITOU: This is the first time we have been photographed
            together.

SARAH: [*to* MME DE GOURNAY] Will you hurry please? I can't
            balance here forever.

MME DE G: [*from under the camera*] Why are all the pieces white?

SARAH: That is a secret. Photographs should always be mysterious,
            charged with unexplained drama. Photographs, like life,
            should be full of feeling. Passion, Pitou.

PITOU: I am better at acting enigmatic.

SARAH: In that case, I shall give out an aura of intellectual wist-
            fulness.

MME DE G: But how do you know which pieces are yours?

SARAH: Take the photograph. Not everything can be explained.

                        [MME DE GOURNAY *takes the photograph. The*

magnesium flash explodes. DENUCÉ *cries out.* PITOU
goes to him.]

PITOU: It's only a photograph, Major. We'll take one of you in a
moment.

[DENUCÉ *holds* PITOU*'s hand tightly.*]

SARAH: We must do the solos now, Pitou.

[MME DE GOURNAY *helps* SARAH *into the wheelchair.*
PITOU, *with difficulty, pulls away from* DENUCÉ *and
goes to the camera.*]

Concentrate on the eyes. I can convey more with my
eyes than most playwrights can with an entire scene. [*to*
MME DE GOURNAY] Put on some music, bright and
sparkling. From a ballet. That'll make the choice simpler
for you. And let us be quick, Pitou. Capture this gaiety.
Important the public believe me truly restored. Publicity
is all illusion.

[MME DE GOURNAY *winds up the phonograph and
puts on a record. From the phonograph* SARAH*'s voice is
heard.*]

VOICE: 'Why? Do you want to know why, Armand? Because
there are moments when I lose myself in that dream.'

SARAH: Why have you put that on?

MME DE G: A mistake, I'm sorry —

VOICE: 'Because there are days when I am weary of the life I
lead and imagine another, because in the midst of my
turbulent existence —'

SARAH: [*to* MME DE GOURNAY] Give it to me.

[MME DE GOURNAY *brings the record to* SARAH, *who
breaks it.*]

People will say that was recorded after my death. You've
spoiled my mood.

MME DE G: I'm terribly sorry.

SARAH: I am exhausted now. No more of this. Pitou, go and see if
there's any post. I want letters, plays, poetry, offers.

PITOU: The solos —

SARAH: Go and see if anyone wants me.

[PITOU *goes.*]

DENUCÉ: Pitou, Pitou —
MME DE G: He's going for the post. [*to* SARAH] He's very attached to
            Pitou. They hold hands.
DENUCÉ: Wants me to remember. Hurts to remember.
SARAH: Yes. Memory is painful. I hate the past. My voice then,
            those words 'my turbulent existence' suddenly evoked a
            hideous mirage of memories. My life has been shot with
            thunder and lightning. Yes, it seems now that my life
            was fiction, a dream. The true substance was the time I
            spent upon the stage acting, and in rehearsing when I
            was not acting, fourteen, fifteen hours a day. Looking
            back that is all that seems to matter now. The whirlwind
            of dates, the titles, the gleaming swords, the fireworks,
            the men of genius and the clever men, the honours,
            smiles, prayers and tears, they do not count. My voyages
            round the world, up and down the provinces of every
            country, my bankruptcies, my vast fees and fortunes, the
            despair, the joy, all these do not count. I was the greatest
            lover in the world. Kings and princes competed for my
            favours. I earned and lost millions upon millions. Oscar
            Wilde laid an armful of lilies at my feet. I enslaved cities.
            In London 100,000 admirers filled three volumes with
            their signatures on my birthday. The streets of New
            York were blocked by my admirers. The Prince of Wales
            allowed me to dress him as my dead lover in *Fédora* and
            he lay upon the stage so that he could say he played a
            scene with me. Everything I did or said was repeated,
            written down, distorted. I think of that part of my life
            and a great clamour arises: applause, sobs, whistling
            trains, steamers screaming in the fog, a patchwork of all
            countries, a babel of all tongues, shouts of enthusiasm, a
            great litany of worship. To the world I was earth, air,
            fire, water. Vapour producing vapour. My marriage,
            lovers, passions, are like my sculpture, my painting, my
            playwriting: these were the sideshows. But the star
            attraction, the profound fact of my life was that I acted
            on a stage. I want to act now. I must act again. My reality
            is the creation of illusion. I hate the past. Memory is a

curse.

DENUCÉ: Sa-rah, Sa-rah, Sa-rah —

SARAH: Stop that. It makes you dribble. Call me when Pitou returns.

[MME DE GOURNAY *starts to wheel* SARAH *off.*]

I can manage. Stay with the Major. What are you teaching him to knit now?

MME DE G: A pair of socks.

SARAH: That is in very bad taste.

[SARAH *exits.* MME DE GOURNAY *resumes the work with the newspaper cuttings.*]

DENUCÉ: Spring now, no more rain, hate the rain, and the mud. Can't keep the wounds dry. Woke from a dream.

MME DE G: You weren't asleep.

DENUCÉ: Glory, she said. Thunderclouds —

MME DE G: Stop that now. You're talking nonsense again. Do your knitting. You mustn't upset yourself.

DENUCÉ: Her voice —

MME DE G: Concentrate on what you're doing.

DENUCÉ: Want Pitou.

MME DE G: As soon as he gets back.

DENUCÉ: Wants me to tell him the story.

MME DE G: Yes, yes, very nice —

DENUCÉ: Teaches me to make things —

MME DE G: So do I —

DENUCÉ: Snip, snip, snip, snip —

MME DE G: Go on with your knitting.

[*He knits. She cuts out and pastes.*]

There's a war on, and they have nothing else to write about but an old woman giving recitations. And she only did it because she wanted the publicity. The soldiers come second. Didn't you hear her? 'I reminded the world of my existence.' Well, of course you heard her. Impossible not to. I don't know why she bothers with the telephone. They'd have heard her in Paris without one.

[PITOU *comes running in, brandishing an unopened envelope.*]

PITOU: Where is she? We've had a letter. A New York postmark.

An offer, I've no doubt. I'm almost too frightened to open it. My hands are trembling. [*He tears it open.*] Yes, yes, from New York! [*He reads, bursts out laughing then stops abruptly.*] This is a disaster. [*He puts the letter in his pocket.*] Say nothing.

MME DE G: About what, what is it?

PITOU: Say nothing.

> [PITOU *paces.* DENUCÉ *sings a snatch of 'The Night-ingale Song'.*]

MM DE G: That's right, Major, you sing, he laughs, and I cut out pieces from the newspaper to paste them in a book. [*She reads:*] 'Troops cheer our greatest actress', 'An inspiring visit.' The newspapers are full of catastrophe but you sing, he laughs, and I cut out items favourable to my employer. [*She reads:*] 'She is a woman whose courage is infectious.'

PITOU: I wish you'd catch some of it.

> [*Somewhere the handbell rings.* MME DE GOURNAY *shudders; after a moment she rises and goes.* PITOU *sits by* DENUCÉ.]

So, Fido, How's the knitting coming along? Must keep the boys at the front warm.

> [DENUCÉ *takes hold of* PITOU*'s hand.*]

Please, Fido, you must stop doing that. People will talk. Let go, there's a good chap. Please. [DENUCÉ *keeps a tight hold.*] Well, I suspect we all need a bit of comfort. As a matter of fact, I welcome a bit of hand-holding. I have a very unpleasant task to perform. We've had an offer. But what an offer. I suppose I have to tell her. Whether I do or not, she'll find out.

> [MME DE GOURNAY *wheels in* SARAH. DENUCÉ *immediately lets go of* PITOU*'s hand and half stands, smiling devotedly at* SARAH.]

Down boy, down boy, down.

SARAH: What's all this about a letter from New York?

PITOU: [*to* MME DE GOURNAY] I told you not to say —

SARAH: Read me the letter, Pitou.

PITOU: [*to* MME DE GOURNAY] Why not take the Major for a

walk? [*to* DENUCÉ] Fido, go for a walk.
> [DENUCÉ *grabs hold of* PITOU'*s hand.*]

There you are, you see? He won't let go of my paw.

SARAH: I want to hear what's in the letter.
> [PITOU *nods sharply to* MME DE GOURNAY, *who goes.*]

PITOU: Leave us; down boy, down. Stay. Stay.

SARAH: Why are you so cruel to him? Read me the letter, Pitou.
> [PITOU *tries to free his hand then pulls away from* DENUCÉ.]

PITOU: That's a good boy.
> [PITOU *takes out the letter.*]

SARAH: Is it an offer?

PITOU: Yes.

SARAH: I knew it, I knew it. All this publicity was bound to bear fruit. Read it to me, read it to me. What sort of offer?

PITOU: From America.

SARAH: Yes, yes. They adore me in America.

PITOU: A tour.

SARAH: Wonderful. I long to cross the ocean again.

PITOU: One problem. [*He reads:*] 'Because of the present hostilities, transfer of funds to France is nigh impossible. You would have to finance your own journey and we would refund you on arrival.' We have not the funds to be refunded.

SARAH: You've become fearfully preoccupied with money. This tour: major cities?

PITOU: And others.

SARAH: What others?

PITOU: Here's the pertinent passage. [*He reads:*] 'But all these dates are conditional upon the aforementioned circus offer which we strongly recommend, for we believe we could negotiate a very high fee. She would, of course, appear in what is called the star spot, that is to say, after the lions and before the elephants.'
> [*A long silence.* SARAH *is absolutely still. Very slowly she wheels herself off.*]

DENUCÉ: Don't go —

PITOU: My point of view precisely.

DENUCÉ: Snip-snip, snip-snip. Please.

> [*Pause.* PITOU *takes up a double sheet of newspaper, folds it carefully, then picks up the scissors and begins to cut.*]

PITOU: Snip-snip, snip-snip, snip-snip-snip.

DENUCÉ: Snip-snip-snip, snip, snip-snip.

> [DENUCÉ *smiles.* PITOU *finishes cutting then unfolds the paper which he has cut into a row of joined figures in the shape of elephants.* DENUCÉ, *smiling, applauds slowly.*]

> [*Lights fade to blackout.*]

> [*In the darkness, voices are heard from the phonograph:*]

OFFICER: 'Scarpio is dead!'

> [*Angry shouts.*]

SPOLETTA: 'Ah! Devil! I will send you to join your dead lover!'

SARAH: 'I go willingly.'

> [*The sound of the phonograph hissing and clicking, and of a solitary slow hand-clap.*]

> [*Lights.*]

> [PITOU *is at the phonograph.* DENUCÉ, *wearing a silly smile, applauds slowly.* MME DE GOURNAY *enters.* PITOU *stops the phonograph.*]

MME DE G: I never thought anyone could cry so much. She seems to be crying her life away, as though the tears were dousing the embers.

PITOU: I swear that's a quotation. Racine? Phaedra. She's been talking to you, I can tell —

MME DE G: She even embraced me. I resisted at first but then gave way. It was the first time she ever seemed to need me. She buried her face in my neck. My collar is still wet. 'A circus, a circus, God help me a circus,' she said. 'I must have sinned. I'm being punished.'

> [PITOU *laughs.*]

PITOU: Excellent, splendid, wonderful. That's that. I'll make arrangements for our return to Paris. The last journey.

Thank God. We shall all die in our beds. And about time.

> [*He does a little dance of joy.* SARAH *wheels herself in.* PITOU *is still. Silence.*]

She is no longer crying.

SARAH: Bring me my jewels.

> [PITOU *is suddenly alarmed.*]

PITOU: Why? What for?

SARAH: You know why.

PITOU: Do nothing rash. Pause. Consider. What you need is a play. And who knows, there may be a playwright at this moment —

> [SARAH *explodes with real venom.*]

SARAH: Don't mention that word playwright to me. It's not so long ago that they were beating a path to my door with their crass melodramas. On their knees they came, pilgrims to the shrine, begging me to read their grubby little manuscripts, praying to the Good God that I should condescend to speak their unspeakable lines. I have put vast fortunes into the pockets of playwrights. Where would they be without me? I guaranteed production, I guaranteed success. Don't mention playwrights to me. They do their work, if you call it work, and then they lose interest. And we actors have to perform night after night, year in, year out, while playwrights disport themselves in Monte Carlo. And do they visit us? How often have you seen a playwright in a dressing-room? And if they do make an enquiry after their puppets, you may be certain it is only to ask whether or not the house was full. Royalties, that's all that interests them. Playwrights are not artists, they are businessmen.

PITOU: Nevertheless, you cannot do without them —

SARAH: And ask them to cut a line, a precious word, and one would think one was asking Our Lord to revise the Sermon on the Mount. Don't speak to me of playwrights. And where are they now I am alone and in jeopardy? Where? Not one has the wit to write me a part in which I sit or stand. [PITOU *tries to interrupt.*] Playwrights! God help us when audiences pay to see plays instead of actors in plays. They are nothing without us. Playwrights need actors. Playwrights are pimps.

PITOU: Granted, but they are also a necessary evil.

SARAH: Circus acts can do without them.

[*Silence.*]

PITOU: So it's the circus, is it?

SARAH: Bring me my jewels.

PITOU: It's a high price to pay.

SARAH: You do not know the half of it.

PITOU: I hate the circus.

SARAH: You are not alone. I hate tightrope walkers and bare-back riders. I have never laughed at clowns. A circus is cruelty to animals, and they are asking me to be an animal-act, a one-legged human who spouts poetry. I hate cruelty to animals. I regret playing Lady Macbeth in a leopard skin. I always got a laugh on 'Out, out damn'd spot'.

PITOU: Let me send a cable: 'Your offer totally unacceptable —'

SARAH: Give me my jewels —

PITOU: Why? Why? Why?

SARAH: Better a circus than a charitable institution for cripples.

PITOU: You're certain of that, are you?

SARAH: I have been trying to imagine what it'll be like. One would have to wait outside the tent, listening to the roar of the lions and the cracking of whips. One would hear too, the circus band, all trombones and euphoniums, like a constipated gorilla straining for relief.

PITOU: Yes, yes, and think of the smells.

SARAH: Yes, animal manure and human sweat. But perhaps the elephants would trumpet a protest. At having to follow me. I adore elephants. They are the only beasts on this planet who instinctively understand that life is unbearably funny and unbearably sad. That is why they look the way they do. They know the meaning of humiliation.

MME DE G: May I add my voice?

PITOU: Is your collar dry?

MME DE G: I had a dream last night of childhood. My father took me once to a circus, the only time I've ever been. And what impressed me most was the trapeze artist, a young woman with bright red hair. She was thrown between two men, somersaulting, cavorting, twisting and turning. She had muscular legs, I remember. I dreamed of her last night. I saw her falling from a height and there was no safety net.

SARAH: That is your dream, it has nothing to do with me. Dreams are always personal.

PITOU: You will not be reproached for declining the offer.

[*Pause.*]

SARAH: I want you to photograph me. Solo. Let it be harsh and cruel. Let it reveal acceptance. Let it show me staring into the camera, confronting my own image. The world has become impervious to mutilation. So must I. I have been supported by crutches, by self-deception, by gazing lovingly into distorting mirrors. No more lies. No more lip-service to survival. That does not mean I shan't, from time to time, suffer panic, or despair, or harbour thoughts of self-destruction, or need comfort, or escape into a fantastical garden of sweet scented flowers. But I determine from this moment to use reality, to take affliction into my being and transform it into triumph. With my will I shall use truth and terror to fuel my fragile presence. Let the photograph be life-like. I am. I shall be.

[*Silence.*]

PITOU: You are an actress, not an act.

[*Silence.*]

SARAH: Give me my jewels.

[PITOU *goes to a cupboard and unlocks it.*]

Madame de Gournay?

MME DE G: Yes?

SARAH: Thank you for comforting me.

[PITOU *brings* SARAH *her jewel box.*]

[*to* MME DE GOURNAY] Come. Sit by me. We will sort the jewels.

[PITOU *returns to* DENUCÉ.]

PITOU: Fido, I'll teach you to cut patterns out of newspapers.

SARAH: We will sell enough to settle my debts, and to buy one first-class passage on an ocean liner. And two in steerage.

PITOU: I have lost the day.

SARAH: We must rid ourselves of sad jewels, of sombre stones. Jewels ought to be happy. Sell these diamonds. I detest diamonds. Hard and unfeeling. To feel. That is paramount. Diamonds remind me of those who smile with eyes of bayonets. Sell them.

PITOU: Instead of bits and pieces, allow me to say it would be better to rid oneself of one grand possession.

SARAH: I have already done that. I have lost a leg.

PITOU: I mean the villa at Belle-Île.

SARAH: Never. I would rather lose all I have than sell Belle-Île. One day, Madame de Gournay, I shall take you to Belle-Île.

MME DE G: Is it very beautiful?

SARAH: At night, when the Furies plague me, I think of Belle-Île and I am comforted. Terrible to become attached to a single spot on this earth, to cliffs and sea, to the wild, bleak skies. No. Sell the diamonds. And the amethysts and bloodstone and garnets. But not Belle-Île. Keep the burnt topaz. It's deep and variegated, and much finer than yellow diamonds. It was given me by a king.

        [She tries not to cry.]

MME DE G: And these pearls?

SARAH: No. Not the pearls. I adore pearls. This one was slipped into my hand by a man on the railway station in Vienna. I tried to thank him, but he scuttled away and disappeared into a third-class carriage. How curious people are.

PITOU: Yes. How curious.

        [He laughs.]

MME DE G: Perhaps he couldn't afford the pearl. Perhaps it was a sacrifice.

SARAH: The world is very unjust. Thank God. Pitou, take my photograph. I have done what had to be done.

        [She shuts the jewel box. PITOU goes to the camera. SARAH takes up pen and pad.]

And you're to have this made. Remember, in a circus people sit in a circle so I must be protected on all sides. Find carpenters. Get the Major to help. It will be good for him. We will rehearse.

PITOU: You are determined.

SARAH: I must learn my lines.

[PITOU *takes the photograph. The magnesium flash explodes.* DENUCÉ *cries out and begins to shudder.*]

MME DE G: The Major —

SARAH: Get his medicine —

[MME DE GOURNAY *goes for his medicine.* PITOU *runs to* DENUCÉ.]

PITOU: It's all right, it's all right —

SARAH: Give him his sedative —

MME DE G: He'll never swallow it —

PITOU: Leave the spoon, give me the bottle. Hold him.

[SARAH *wheels herself to* DENUCÉ, *takes his face in her hands and holds him tightly.*]

SARAH: Now.

[PITOU *feeds* DENUCÉ *from the bottle.*]

Swallow, no matter how bitter. [*to* MME DE GOURNAY] Something to take away the taste.

[MME DE GOURNAY *finds a sweet and gives it to* DENUCÉ. SARAH *holds him until he is calm.*]

MME DE G: He remembers the horror.

[PITOU *simulates his expression of horror.*]

SARAH: It would be better if we were born each day afresh. Without memory. Constantly I remember my roles, beings divided from me, quite separate, independent creations, yet more real than — [*She breaks off.*] It is the same for him. He is a man divided. His reality is not of the present. The cure is unity and acceptance. [*Pause.*] What do doctors of the mind know? Suffer the sick to come unto actors.

[*She smiles at* DENUCÉ, *who is more or less calm.* MME DE GOURNAY *helps him to a chair and settles him.*]

MME DE G: He's calmer now.

SARAH: I must work, I must study, I must lie in my coffin, I

must, as they say, put together my act. My next trick will
be impossible.

> [MME DE GOURNAY *wheels her off.* PITOU *watches
> them go.*]

PITOU: Insanity, I suppose, should engage our compassion. *Sic
transit gloria mundi.* Doesn't she know one should never
pull an elephant by the tail? Once, I remember —

DENUCÉ: Told me her name. Sssssss . . .

PITOU: What?

DENUCÉ: Bombardment number three sector continuing. A sign.
Slapped. Slapped me. Twins. Double Life.

PITOU: Yes, yes, her memoirs — why? —

DENUCÉ: Didn't ask to be born. Blackness and gun smoke. Awful
noise. Lost my button. Awful pain. [*He touches his head.*]
Silence. No feeling. A sign.

> [PITOU *begins to take notes.*]

She and I, alone. Her voice. A great distance. Sunless
regions. Piercing darkness. Voice of gold. Felt her
hands, saw her eyes, blazing gems, heard my heart, a
pounding gun. Thought I'd entered a room. Saw someone I'd lost, someone I'd loved, someone from whom the
world divided me. A child spoke. Saw Phaedra,
Marguerite Gau—, Napoleon's son, Duke of — Duke of
— Two lost children. Words. Unfamiliar. Stirring.
Other worlds. No sense of being. Only glory. Glory.
Gave a sign. No one there. A shaft of sunlight.

> [*He hums 'The Nightingale Song'.* PITOU *continues to
> write for a moment, then stops.*]

PITOU: These are the mysteries. We have a grave responsibility.
'You should've seen her,' we'll say, and the youngsters
will shrug and answer, 'We've seen better.' [*Pause.*] We
are nothing without her.

> [*He is consumed by sudden and dreadful rage.*]

She's an old hag!

> [DENUCÉ *smiles and continues to hum.* PITOU *goes.*]

[*Blackout.*]

[*Lights.*]

[MME DE GOURNAY *is stitching a black doublet, trimmed with gold.* SARAH *lies in the coffin, softly murmuring her lines.* PITOU *enters.* MME DE GOURNAY *gestures for him to go.*]

MME DE G: She's learning her lines —

PITOU: Leave us.

MME DE G: But she said —

PITOU: Leave us.

[MME DE GOURNAY *goes.* PITOU *paces energetically, working himself up.*]

I'm not going to apologize for disturbing you, because I feel obliged to make one last effort to dissuade you from leaving these shores. I am against a long transatlantic crossing. You'll be exhausted before you arrive. If you arrive. The Bosche is no respecter of persons or personages. His torpedoes are merciless. Do I make myself clear? I am against going to America.

[*He calms down a little.*]

So what's the alternative? A return to Paris, a stately life of honours, admiration and work. What work, you ask? A play, I reply. Don't get excited. You will not have to wait indefinitely.

[*He takes out his notebook.*]

I am now ready to inform you that I, Pitou, am about to put pen to paper. I am going to write you a play. [*Pause.*] All I need is encouragement. As who does not? [*Pause.*] It is the story, not of your past, but of your present. If I tell you that my play begins with Major Denucé's words — [*He consults his notebook.*] 'Above the knee,' you will understand. Throughout you will be in a wheelchair or helped to stand by loving — by attentive attendants. I have been keeping notes, recording things said and done over these past months. [*He reads:*] 'Then I shall have plays written for me in which I sit on a throne.' Well. Here we are. And why not? You will order Denucé to wash — I'll die of septicaemia, such blackness — and we will see you trying to walk, visiting the battlefields, carried in your chair. We will see you inspiring the wounded and the dying. I have thought of a marvellous scene, two marvellous scenes with the Major. We will see him stirred by your presence. We will hear in his own words what that meant — [*He reads:*] — 'She and I, alone. Her voice,' and so on and so forth. I have all the notes. And you will ask, 'What will become of me? What was the purpose of all that pain?' But here let art command reality. If it pleased you we could collaborate. Let us write a different final act. No circus. But my play with a happy ending. Our play.

> [*He sits near the coffin.*]

Do not sell your jewels. If it's money that's worrying you, allow me to say that I have been prudent. I have made investments. I am in receipt of a modest income. To which you are welcome. [*Pause.*] I apologize for being forever abrasive. Once you said I was a different person when we were alone. This is because — [*Pause.*] Allow me to say. [*Pause.*] There is no need to reply now, but — [*Pause.*] I should like nothing more in this life than to care for you until — [*Pause.*] I am fully aware that I am not the most presentable of men, but I have such for you — such — I have profound feelings. [*Pause.*] I am your servant. [*Pause.*] I would not regard it an insult if, for one reason or another, you did not deem it fitting to use my name. Sarah Pitou is not — [*Pause.*] Once I came into your room. You were lying as you are now. Do you remember? Were you alone in this coffin? Was I imagining? [*Pause.*] I am able to put from my mind your present disability. I see you as I first saw you — overwhelming and divine. I am your servant.

> [*He leans very close to the coffin, whispers, and seems about to climb in on top of her.*]

Shall I? Shall I?

> [*He waits for an answer.* SARAH *snores.* PITOU *rushes out.* SARAH *continues to snore.* MME DE GOURNAY *returns, sits and resumes her stitching.* MME DE GOURNAY *whistles.* SARAH *stops snoring.*]

[*Blackout.*]

[*Hammering.*]

[*Lights.*]

[*The* OLD CARPENTER *and the* YOUNG CARPENTER
are at work on the platform. DENUCÉ *is putting finishing
touches to the painted ballustrade.* MME DE GOURNAY
wheels in SARAH.]

MME DE G: Look at what the Major's painted. He has a gift.

SARAH: Good, Major.

DENUCÉ: All done.

SARAH: It's very fine and just what I wanted. You should give an
exhibition in Paris. It's meant to be a ballustrade, not
can-can dancers on a foggy day. But it's excellent. It will
serve our purpose.

MME DE G: And these are the men who made the platform. They're
from the village.

[*The* TWO CARPENTERS *bow. They are horribly
embarrassed and overawed.*]

OLD MAN: Honoured.

SARAH: Show me how the platform runs.

[*The* OLD CARPENTER *nods to the* YOUNG CAR-
PENTER. *They pull the platform this way and that.*]
Splendid. Now you must fit the ballustrade.

[*The* OLD CARPENTER *nods to the* YOUNG CAR-
PENTER, *who takes the ballustrade from* DENUCÉ *and
begins to fit it around the platform so that the stool and
most of the pillar are concealed.*]

OLD MAN: Would you sign this.

[*He offers her a photograph.*]

SARAH: Joan of Arc. A favourite role. Did you see me play the
part?

OLD MAN: No. It's just that my mother was born in Domrémy.

SARAH: My interpretation of Joan of Arc is not meant to remind
you of your mother. Never mind. Fit the ballustrade.

[*Having signed the photograph, she returns it to the* OLD

CARPENTER, *who helps the* YOUNG CARPENTER *fit
the ballustrade.*]

MME DE G: It's nearly time.

SARAH: I am nervous. Why should I be so frightened? Perhaps
it's the presence of those two men. One stranger consti-
tutes an audience. I can hardly catch my breath. Will I
remember? Do I know the lines? I have played the part a
dozen times but still I — [*She stops.*] Where will you sit?

MME DE G: Here?

SARAH: Good. And the Major?

MME DE G: By the phonograph.

SARAH: The men must complete the circle. Is my make-up all
right?

MME DE G: Perfect.

SARAH: You must forget I'm old.

MME DE G: Of course.

SARAH: Having to say that betrays my lack of confidence. I feel
as though all over again I'm making my debut.

MME DE G: I feel nothing but excitement.

SARAH: And, Major, you must make no noise while I speak.
Promise?

DENUCÉ: Promise.

SARAH: And no dribbling.

DENUCÉ: No.

SARAH: We must all lose a sense of ourselves.

MME DE G: We will. We will.

SARAH: What is Pitou up to? Why do I put up with him?

MME DE G: He's preparing a speech, an introduction. Shall I tell
Pitou to begin?

SARAH: Very well. And take off the platform so I can prepare.
And do not say, 'Break a leg.'
[*She wheels herself off.*]

MME DE G: [*to the* TWO CARPENTERS] Take the platform off please.
She will tell you when to bring it on.
[*The* TWO CARPENTERS *pull the platform off.* MME
DE GOURNAY *winds up the phonograph, selects a
record and places it on the turntable.* DENUCÉ *has come
to her.*]

DENUCÉ: Dance, dance.

MME DE G: No, no, no. I was never very good.

DENUCÉ: Yes. Dance. Please.

MME DE G: No. I was in the corps-de-ballet, never a soloist. I was not naturally turned-out. Now go and sit down.

> [*As* DENUCÉ *goes to his chair he catches sight of the unseen* SARAH.]

DENUCÉ: Crossed herself.

> [*He demonstrates.*]

MME DE G: Go and sit there. [*She calls:*] Are you ready?

SARAH: [*off*] Ready.

> [MME DE GOURNAY *calls to* PITOU:]

MME DE G: We're ready! We're ready!

> [MME DE GOURNAY *and* DENUCÉ *take their seats.* PITOU *enters. He wears white tie and tails and the false nose of a clown. He makes clawing movements and roars like a lion. He gives a hand-cue to* DENUCÉ, *who puts on the record — something by Offenbach.*]

PITOU: Lady and gentleman! Welcome! Welcome to Sarah's Circus. Admission free, children and invalids half price. Tonight you are privileged, nay uniquely privileged, to witness before your very eyes, the eighth wonder of the world — I am your guide into uncharted territory, that country where — [*He lowers his voice:*] — the divine queen-goddess is determined to continue her life as though neither time nor the surgeon's knife has scarred her. [*He raises his voice again:*] For, she belongs, lady and gentleman, to that tribe who crawl from their dens at night, who prowl and strut and stalk their prey in darkness and like moths are drawn to bright, bright light. I mean of course, the Theatre Tribe, for our queen-goddess is an actress, Queen of the land of illusion, the kingdom of dreams. Tonight, and on succeeding nights, until the oceans turn to sawdust, you are privileged to witness the rehearsal of an amazing act —

SARAH: [*off*] Get on with it, Pitou.

PITOU: Now you hear the roar of the lions and smell the filth of animals. And you are entitled to ask with the poet, 'Is man no more than this?'

    [*The phonograph runs slow.*]

Take it off, take it off!

    [DENUCÉ *stops the record.*]

Lady and gentleman, I give you the only, the one and
only — thank God — the one and only Sarah Barnum!

    [DENUCÉ *applauds and stamps his feet.*]

MME DE G: Not yet, Major, not yet.

    [*The* TWO CARPENTERS *pull in the platform. On the
    platform sits* SARAH, *cloaked and hooded.* PITOU *pulls
    her into the centre, then goes to the camera and covers
    himself with the cloth.* SARAH *stands, holding on to the
    truncated pillar with one hand.*]

SARAH: Ladies and Gentlemen, I give you a speech from one of
my greatest roles: Hamlet, Prince of Denmark.

    [*She throws off her cloak. She is dressed in an inky black
    doublet and wears a boyish wig.*]

'O, what a rogue and peasant slave am I!
Is it not monstrous that this player here,
But in a fiction, in a dream of passion,
Could force his soul so to his own conceit
That from her working all his visage wann'd,
Tears in his eyes, distraction in 's aspect,
A broken voice, and his whole function suiting
With forms to his conceit? and all for nothing!
For Hecuba!
What's Hecuba to him, or he to Hecuba,
That he should weep for her? What would he do,
Had he the motive and the cue for passion
That I have? He would drown —'

    [*She makes a great sweeping gesture, knocks over the
    ballustrade so that she is fully revealed for the first time,
    balancing on one leg, holding on to the truncated pillar.
    The* YOUNG CARPENTER *laughs but the* OLD
    CARPENTER *gives a severe look to silence him. Her
    concentration is disturbed by the accident, but she
    continues hesitantly:*]

'He would drown — he would drown the stage with tears
— cleave, cleave, the general — the general ear with
horrid speech, make mad the guilty — make mad the
guilty — confound the ignorant — appal the free — Yet
I! Yet I! Yet I!'

> [*She cannot remember. But she stands in a glorious pose.*
> MME DE GOURNAY *is lost in wonder.* DENUCÉ *smiles
> his vacant smile and begins to applaud slowly. The*
> YOUNG CARPENTER *watches open-mouthed; the* OLD
> CARPENTER *wipes away tears. Under the camera cloth,*
> PITOU's *whole body shakes with weeping; or he could
> be laughing.* SARAH *stands perfectly still, maintaining
> the pose on one leg, arm raised, head held high,
> triumphant.*]

> [*The lights fade.*]

> [*Blackout.*]

THE NIGHTINGALE SONG

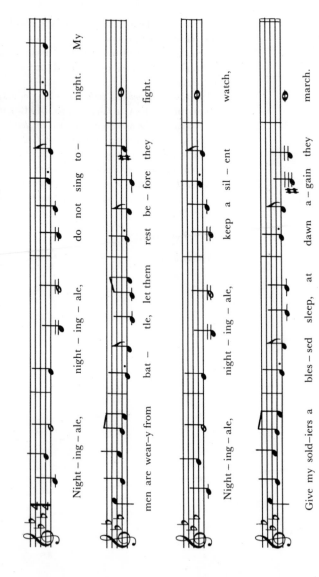

Night – ing – ale, night – ing – ale, do not sing to – night. My

men are wear-y from bat – tle, let them rest be – fore they fight.

Night – ing – ale, night – ing – ale, keep a sil – ent watch,

Give my sold-iers a bles – sed sleep, at dawn a – gain they march.